SERIES EDITOR

Dr. Sally Monsour

Professor of Music Education
Georgia State University
Atlanta

Integrating Music with Other Studies

by Dr. Mary Ann Mulligan

Professor of Music Education
Georgia State University
Atlanta

Classroom Music Enrichment Units

THE CENTER FOR APPLIED RESEARCH IN EDUCATION, INC.
521 FIFTH AVENUE, NEW YORK, N.Y. 10017

The Center for Applied
Research in Education, Inc.
New York

Library of Congress Cataloging in Publication Data

Mulligan, Mary Ann.
Integrating music with other studies.
(Classroom Music Enrichment Units)

Bibliography and discography: p.
1. School music–Instruction and study. 2. Music in education. I. Title. II. Series.
MT1.M92 372.8'7'044 75-30691
ISBN 0-87628-218-4

Printed in the United States of America

About This Handbook

Integrating Music with Other Studies includes a series of lesson ideas that suggest the numerous possibilities of noticing how our world is more related than unrelated, more whole than fragmented. The ideas are general enough to be used in a variety of learning settings. Most of them can also be used at several grade levels. While the material is directed primarily to the elementary classroom teacher, it should also help the music specialist supplement the regular program at the elementary and junior high school levels.

The way musical sounds are commonly organized differs from one culture to another, from one time in history to another, and from one age group to another. And yet, music will always include patterns, repetitions, contrasts, and the relationships among them. It is the purpose of this handbook to explore these relationships and to give ideas for using music in the larger context of many other subjects found in school.

As in all curriculum studies teachers should be concerned with both the process and the product. The integration of music will be more effective if these two concepts are clearly understood. Key words that will serve this end are:

Processes:	combining	*Products:*	balance
	classifying		contrast
	associating		pattern
	relating		design
	organizing		unity
	repeating		variety
	sequencing		

The ideas in this handbook fall into two categories: (1) enrichment activities while studying subjects other than music, or (2) musical experiences based on concepts similar to those in other subjects. The subjects included are social studies, science, mathematics, and language arts. Each of these is explored for convergence and interrelationships.

Where suggested recordings are not available in the school or district collection, the public library should be checked. The children

may also bring recordings from home. Many suggestions incorporate standard collections such as the *Bowmar Orchestral Library, RCA Adventures in Music,* and the music series of well-known publishers.

Hopefully, the ideas in this handbook will stimulate your creativity and help you devise your own analogous lessons using music with other subjects. A key to developing interest in music is the involvement of children as well in experiences where their own creative ideas are required. Musical insights discovered in interrelationships will result in the excitement that music can generate, thus enriching the lives of children.

Mary Ann Mulligan

Contents

Rich music resources should be extendable; that is, they should be used to integrate learnings in music with learnings in language development, math, science, etc. This does not *mean that music should become the means for teaching reading, addition, or the alphabet, but rather that learnings in all areas should occur simultaneously and reinforce each other.*

Fred Willman *

1

Integrating Music with Social Studies

The social studies show man's relation to man. The vocabulary commonly used reveals many generalizations that can be contrasted with or related to music. The lesson ideas in this first section explore some of the possible interrelationships. These techniques and strategies are merely suggestions and can be easily adapted to other ideas in both music and social studies.

Concepts considered here are grouped under three areas: our world and its peoples, our physical environment, and our economic environment. Ideas are provided under each grouping for both primary and intermediate grades.

EXPLORING CONCEPTS RELATED TO OUR WORLD AND ITS PEOPLES

People differ according to customs, family ties, occupations, traditions, and historical periods. They also differ as a result of geographic, rural or urban, location. The relationship of music to topics studied in the social sciences can be viewed in various ways. One way is stylistic. Another way is to use the topic to suggest material for

* "Individualizing Music Instruction," *Insights Into Open Education,* 6, No. 6 (March 1974) (Grand Forks: Center for Teaching and Learning, University of North Dakota), 3.

original compositions. For instance, though each is distinctive, all cities share certain common problems and characteristics. Children will enjoy identifying these characteristics, how various composers express them, and how they themselves can manipulate sound to express urban concepts.

Early Childhood

The following lesson outlines include ideas for teaching the concepts of tribe, farmer, and explorer. Once you have tried several of these, you will think of many other ideas for using music to develop and enhance concepts relating to our world and its peoples.

- **The Concept of Tribe**

Tribe: a social group of people held together by ties of some sort such as family, geography, or tradition.

1. Tell the children that people differ according to customs of a certain time or certain place. Music also differs according to style, for it is the expression of people from different times and places. The style of a certain piece of music can be discovered if we know the family ties, or traditions, of the people from which it originates.
2. Play a recording of "Blowing in the Wind" (Bob Dylan, *The Concert for Bangladesh,* Apple Recordings, STCX3385); or "This Old Guitar" (John Denver, *Back Home Again,* RCA, CPL1-0548). Ask the children to notice that folk music usually has a singer accompanied by only a few instruments such as the guitar, piano, and percussion.
3. Play a recording of a brief orchestral work such as an excerpt from Howard Hanson's "Merry Mount Suite" (*RCA Adventures in Music,* Gr. 3, Vol. 1). Ask the children to notice orchestral instruments, and the absence of singer and lyrics. This music is in a different style from the first recording.
4. Study the four families of instruments in the orchestra—the string, woodwind, brass, and percussion families. Ask the children to identify why the instruments can be grouped together into families —how are they alike and different?
5. Ask the children to bring a favorite record from home, and compare the differences in style or size of performing group among the records brought.

• **The Concept of Farmer**

Farmer: a person who cultivates land or crops, or raises livestock.

1. Talk about the long hours that a farmer works. He has less time than most other people to be free to make music, but he often sings or plays or listens to music. His music-making is usually simple and short, but frequent.

2. Play the musical game, "The Farmer in the Dell." Ask the children how many times the first phrase of words is repeated (*3*). This makes the song easy to remember, and keeps it from being complicated.

3. Sing the "Barnyard Song," an old Kentucky mountain song (Fig. 1). Notice the simple repetitions.

BARNYARD SONG * Kentucky

Fig. 1

• **The Concept of Explorer**

Explorer: a person who travels where few or no other people have travelled before.

1. Explain how explorers are interested in learning about the places to which they travel. An attitude of interest and inquisitiveness is needed to be a successful explorer.

2. Direct the children to have a vicarious exploration experience by making up an original composition, one never before thought of

---

* May be found in *Exploring Music,* Book 2, Holt-Rinehart Pub. and *Heritage Songster,* Wm. C. Brown Pub.

by anyone else! Display a considerable variety of classroom instruments from which they may choose in order to provide the feeling of a strange environment.

Play the following odd-sounding pattern (ostinato) throughout the children's piece. This will provide a unifying element.

3. Play a recording of music by contemporary composers. Then discuss with the children the difficulty of finding new places to explore on the planet earth. Explain how it *is* possible to explore new sounds. Two examples of appropriate new compositions are: "Wind Song" from *Daphne of the Dunes* by Partch (*New Dimensions in Music,* Early Childhood, rec. 6). Tell about this California composer who invented instruments for his twentieth-century music. The ringing and striking sounds are all very unfamiliar until the eerie violin is heard.

"Gesang der Junglinge" ("Song of the Youths," Stockhausen, Columbia, CSP 11613) is a good example of electronic music.

4. Have the children sing songs about explorers. Some may be found in elementary music series books such as:

"Space Travel" (*Exploring Music,* Bk. 2, p. 130)
"Space Explorer" (*Spectrum of Music,* Bk. 3, p. 204)
"Your World" (William Grant Still, *The Magic of Music,* Bk. 6, p. 195)
"Columbus" (*The Magic of Music,* Bk. 3, p. 85)

Middle Childhood

Two ideas for older children stem from the growing awareness of urbanization: population density and slum.

• The Concept of Population Density

Population density: the number of people per unit of area, as a square mile.

1. Lead the children in a discussion. Density means many people in a small space or area. Music is involved with time, not space. We look for density in music by listening for many sounds heard in a short length of time.

2. Play a recording for the children in which the sounds are "sparse," that is, there are not many sounds in the time span of the

piece. The first minute of "Free Country" (Chicago, *Chicago Three*, Columbia, C2-30110) is a good example. Follow this with "Happy 'Cause I'm Going Home" (*Chicago Three*) and ask what makes the second piece more dense. (*Many more instruments, plus several voices, little silence interspersed.*)

Have the children list the different sound sources they hear playing at once—guitars, percussion, voices, horns. Ask if they can mention other things that make this piece sound more dense than the first selection. (*Melodies in close intervals; rhythmic pattern is frequently rapid.*)

Fig. 2 Exploring the concept of slum

• **The Concept of Slum**

Slum: crowded area marked by run-down buildings and poverty.

1. Lead the class in a discussion about the three parts of the definition, i.e., crowded area, run-down buildings, and poverty.

2. Ask for a small volunteer group to compose a soundpiece entitled "The Slum." The three parts of the concept of slum can become the organizing factors. Ask the group to decide how to deal with each, and what relationship each will have to the whole composition.

One possible solution is presented here:

—Choose a time limit for the piece. Most pop tunes run under three minutes, so that may be a good guide.

—Have two performers on the "run-down buildings" part. One performer keeps a steady beat on a low drum while the second performer selects either one of the following rhythmic patterns (ostinati) to be played with a wooden sound, and repeated throughout the piece:

either:

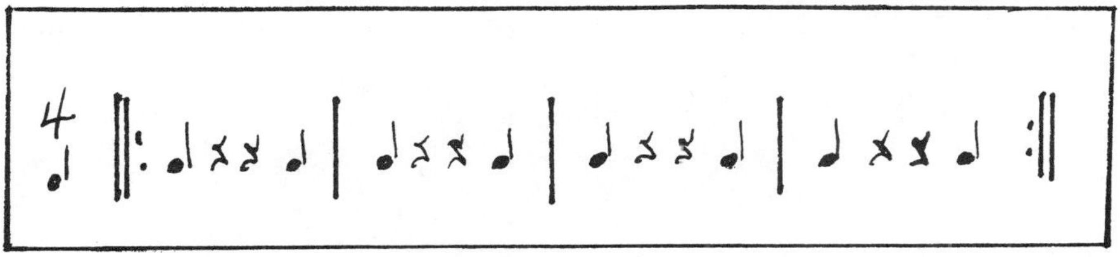

or:

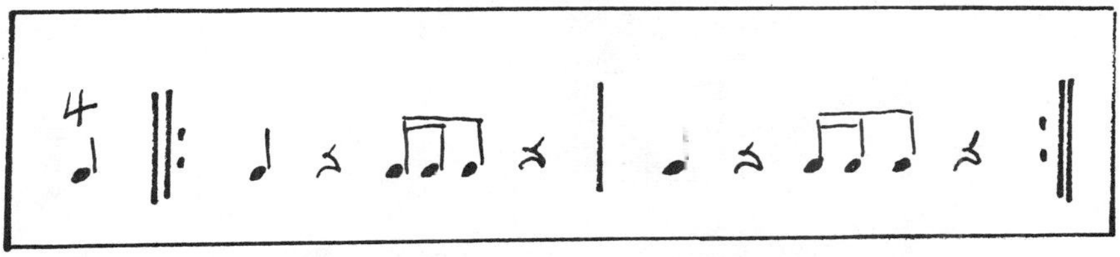

The rests (silences) could denote the deserted buildings, broken windows, or other ideas of emptiness or drabness.

—For "poverty" choose any four instruments, with one performer on each. These four should have a sectional rehearsal to work out their ideas for the expression of their part. A sectional rehearsal is practice time in which one part of the performing group rehearses without the others.

—The preceding two parts may be combined together, or one may follow the other.

—Have the children decide how the third part, the "crowded area," will be depicted. Some of their choices might include having the two parts get louder; having the two parts get faster; adding more sounds.

—After all choices are made, the group practices the piece and records it or plays it for the class.

3. Ask the children to bring to class a recording that they think expresses the combining of several ideas or parts. Lead a class discussion on whether one section seems to predominate over the others. How do all the parts contribute to the whole piece? Did their own musical expression of the three ideas of "crowded area," "run-down buildings," and "poverty" contribute to the whole notion of slum?

EXPLORING CONCEPTS RELATED TO OUR PHYSICAL ENVIRONMENT

Many different kinds of physical terrain affect man, his natural resources, the weather and temperatures, and his adjustment to this environment.

In the following ideas, the musical activities presented tend to enhance the inherent concept of the social science topic or, again, to suggest creative impetus for original classroom compositions. Manipulating sound for an expressive purpose and listening to compositions of successful composers will both develop the children's musical sensitivity and help them understand the human experiences that inspire the creative output of musical artists.

Early Childhood

Topics for younger children include those of desert, plain, mountain, and valley.

• The Concept of Desert

Desert: a very dry place, having little rainfall, and where few plants grow.

1. Discuss with the children the emptiness of the view on a desert, where nothing can be seen but the horizon.
2. Listen to the orchestral selection "On the Steppes of Central Asia" (Borodin, *RCA Adventures in Music,* Gr. 6, Vol. 1). Notice how the opening section has one high, thin pitch to depict the horizon line. Ask the children to observe how little variety the composer introduces at first, which is similar to the slight variation found in a desert where there are few plants and little rainfall.
3. Make up an original composition that expresses a dry and arid place. Choose two "dry" sounds, perhaps wood or rustling paper, for most of the sound material. Choose two other sounds that will be introduced sparingly such as the "annual sparse rainfall" or "lonely tree or plant." Mix the second material with the first to provide the variety you decide your composition needs in order to be interesting. Record the composition for class discussion.
4. Learn one of the following songs about this type of land:

"Saguaro Legend Song" (Amerindian, *Discovering Music Together,* Bk. 4, p. 133)

"Song of the Desert" (Arab chant, *Magic of Music,* Bk. 6, p. 42)

• **The Concept of Plain**

Plain: level land, almost treeless.

1. Make up a composition depicting level land, a plain. What can be done in this composition that will keep the plain from seeming like a desert? Suggest to the children the use of lush timbre (tone quality) for the plain. Choose sounds not as brittle as paper or wood. Put in a distinctive sound infrequently to represent an occasional tree. This will help to clarify the aural difference. Have the children discuss whether deserts have trees.

2. Direct the children in an examination of the classroom songbooks to look for musical notation that seems like it would sound like a plain. Help them to see that the clues they will be looking for are: not much melodic or pitch variety; the presence of rests, especially lengthy ones; much repetition.

3. Play one of the following recordings, or one similar, in which little variety is used in the composition:

"Cushingura" (Jefferson Airplane, *Crown of Creation,* RCA Records)
"Blowin' in the Wind" (Bob Dylan, Apple STXCX 3385)
"Motorboat to Mars" (*Chicago Three,* Columbia, C2-30110)
"Free Country" (*Chicago Three,* above)

Ask the class to compare the last two recordings. The first is totally percussion, while the second uses quietly the flute, piano, and electronic sounds. Ask the children which one seems to portray better their idea of the notion "plain." Either choice is acceptable.

4. Introduce serious orchestral music in order to show that here, also, not many instruments will be used. Suggestions: "In the Village" and "In the Mosque" from *Caucasian Sketches,* Op. 10. (Ippolotov-Ivanov, Vox, VSPS 10/5).

5. Learn to sing songs of the western plains: "My Pony and I" (cowboy song, *Discovering Music Together,* Bk. 4, p. 75), and "My Ranch" (Ramos, *Making Music Your Own,* Bk. 5, p. 166) are two suggestions.

• **The Concept of Mountain**

Mountain: steep land that rises high above the land around it.

1. Discuss with the children the quality of a mountain that we describe as a "peak." In music, composers achieve a sense of "peak" when the piece gets very high, or very fast, or very loud, compared to parts that have been heard before it or that appear after it.

2. Play the recording of Bach's "Little Fugue in G Minor" (*RCA Adventures in Music,* Gr. 6, Vol. 1). Help the children hear the peaks that are evident in the middle of the prelude and at the end of the fugue. At another time, play "Appian Way" from *The Pines of Rome* (Respighi, Everest 3051). The piece builds up from slow, low sounds to a higher pitch, more dynamics, increasing to a great excitement that ends in a peak.

3. Ask the children to bring a recording to play for the class. Some will find examples of a peak in the middle, others will find one at the end of the selection. Lead a discussion on the ways in which composers achieve the feeling of climax in music.

4. Learn the song, "Gonna Build a Mountain," from *Stop the World, I Want to Get Off* (*Silver Burdett Music,* Bk. 6, p. 74).

• The Concept of Valley

Valley: a long, low area usually between hills or mountains.

1. Tell the children that a valley is something different (low) between two things that are similar (high hills).

2. Listen to "Wellington's Victory" from Beethoven's *Victory Symphony,* in which the composer uses the theme, "My Country, 'Tis of Thee." Ask the children to notice the "valleys" of quiet with the theme they will recognize, as contrasted with surrounding "mountains" of sound. They will enjoy the entire movement while they follow Beethoven's use of the British national anthem.

3. Listen at another time time to Schubert's *Symphony No. 8,* First Movement (excerpt, Columbia records CSP 11612). High, full orchestral sounds alternate with the low cello. Ask the children to move their hands above their heads when the high parts are heard, and to show the low valleys by moving their hands down when they notice the low melody.

Middle Childhood

Topics for older children in the area of physical environment are jungle, rain forest, land in contact with the sea such as coast, and

peninsula. With imagination you may choose to use the proposed musical experiences for other topics being studied.

• The Concept of Jungle

Jungle: an area of dense undergrowth or vegetation through which it is difficult to make one's way.

1. Have a group in the class plan an original composition. This group should include in its plans a density of sound, probably smooth and connected (legato), in order to portray intertwining.

2. Choose a limited number of tone colors (timbres), no more than three, for "vegetation." Introduce the sound that is attempting to thread or "struggle" its way through the density. Use pitched sounds such as plucked piano or autoharp strings for both "jungle" and the effort to get through it. Avoid using loudness to depict the struggle, since this might destroy the variety and beauty of the piece.

3. Try these musical elements and concepts:

—pitch: stepwise and repetitious for the density.
—timbre: only three, all pitched.
—duration: longer than shorter sounds, little silence, few tempo or speed changes.
—intensity: use sparingly for the expressiveness of the struggle.

4. After some practice sessions, tape the piece for the class.

• The Concept of Rain Forest

Rain Forest: a tropical woodland where there is very heavy rainfall and dense plant growth.

1. Lead the class in a discussion. Is dense plant growth like population density? How is it similar? How is it different? What is denseness or thickness in music? The word used by musicians is "texture."

2. Have several children in the class create a soundpiece to fit the title "Rain Forest." One performer will portray the rain, which will be heard throughout the entire piece. The tropical woodland will be played with any instruments made of wood. Plucked strings will be suitable for the third thematic idea, dense plant growth. Limit the piece to a short time span, since a rain forest is like a jungle, difficult to move through. We may tire quickly of the struggle! Record the piece, or play it for the class.

Notate the composition by designating original symbols for each of the three thematic ideas above. On a large piece of paper, use these symbols to write down the piece, "The Rain Forest," so that another group in the class can follow the directions and perform its version of the composition at another time.

Discuss musical notation. The prepared paper will contain the musical notation that the next group will "read." Will the students need special reading skills to understand the original writing system? Encourage the group to make their directions clear.

• The Concept of Coast

Coast: land beside the seashore.

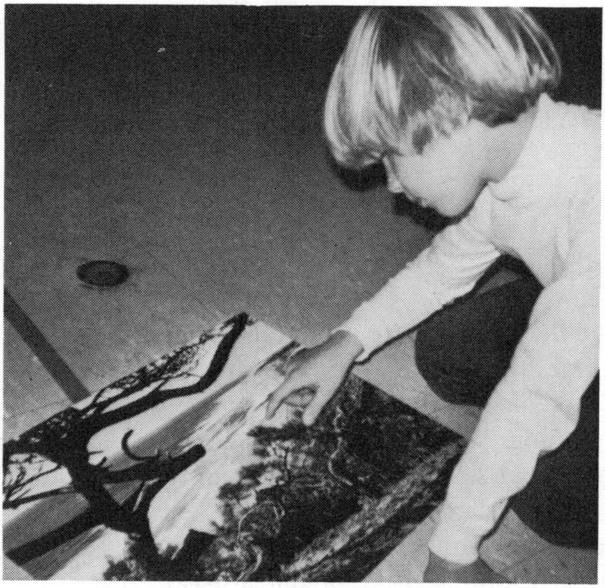

Fig. 3 Exploring the concept of coast

1. Lead the class in a discussion. The concept of coast has two parts, land, and sea or ocean. To have a coast we must have land and sea side by side. In music, the concept of rhythm gives a feeling of motion. Repetition in music expresses repetition in our physical world such as the lapping of waves.

2. Have the children compose a soundpiece called "Coast." Let the piece have two parts, one for the land and one for the sea. A suggested approach: Make an ostinato of steady beats on three or

four tone blocks, or different pitched drums. This will be the land. Select three other rhythmic sounds to portray the moving water, lapping up on the beach. Begin the piece with the ostinato (repeated pattern) alone, for shoreline, then add the sounds for sea. Decide how the piece will end.

3. Play a recording of Smetana's "Furiant" from *The Bartered Bride* (*Discovering Music Together,* Bk. 5). Help the children discover the ABA form of the piece: a rough opening (which might sound like the sea) and a calm, steady middle section (the land).

4. Listen to selections inspired by the sea such as:

"Harbor Vignettes" (Donaldson, *Bowmar,* BOL #53)
"Sea Piece with Birds" (Thomason, *Bowmar,* BOL #70)

5. Sing songs related to the sea. Many elementary music series contain suitable material, including the following:

"Beside the Sea" (Philippine folk song, *Making Music Your Own,* Bk. 5)
"Island in the Sun" (Harry Belafonte, *Spectrum of Music,* Bk. 6)
"Why the Smiling Sea?" (Egyptian, *New Dimensions in Music,* Bk. 5)

• The Concept of Peninsula

Peninsula: a piece of land almost surrounded by water and connected to a larger body of land.

1. Lead the class in a discussion about the concepts of peninsula and island. One is completely surrounded by water and the other one is almost surrounded, for a peninsula is merely connected to a larger body of land. In music, the concept of an accompaniment is analogous. An accompaniment surrounds the singer or soloist. The voice or instrument is like an island, or peninsula, while the guitar, piano, band, or orchestra surround the soloist in a way.

2. Play a recording of a popular artist of today. An example is "Visions" from *Stevie Wonder Innervisions* (Tamla Records, T 326-V1). The acoustic and electric guitars and brass "ebb and flow" before and after the song. In "Morning Has Broken" by Cat Stevens (*Teaser and the Firecat,* Irving Music, A&M SP4313), the piano, guitar, and chorus surround the singer.

NOTE: For a greater challenge, play a jazz recording such as Coleman Hawkins's saxophone solos with full orchestra accompaniment (Everest Records, *Archive of Folk and Jazz,* FS-252).

3. Provide the class with two different styles of music in which

both soloists may be said to have "island" parts: some folk singers on contemporary radio, and concertos heard in concert halls. Two examples are: Olivia Newton-John singing "The River's Too Wide" (MCA-411) and Van Cliburn in *My Favorite Concertos* (RCA Red Seal, RK-1201). In the former, the singing begins without accompaniment; this may be analogous to land. The accompaniment then joins the singer. The song ends as it begins, with no instrument accompaniment.

The soloist in a concerto has "island" parts when he plays alone. He may have "peninsula" parts if some small section of the orchestra accompanies his solo part, attaching his sound to the larger mass of the total orchestra.

EXPLORING CONCEPTS RELATED TO OUR ECONOMIC ENVIRONMENT

Abundance and diversity of resources affect the economic development of different peoples. Resources also dictate the materials possible for creating sounds and producing the music of a particular region.

Early Childhood

Concepts of resources and economic development presented to younger children include those of metals, production, transportation, and even warehouses. You will think of many more.

• The Concept of Metals

Metals: natural resources such as copper, iron, gold, or silver, usually found beneath the earth.

1. Explain to the children that metals have basic similarities (found in the earth), but also, some basic differences. It takes skill to tell the difference between various metals. The symphony orchestra is one of the musical world's "resources" for sound. Within the symphony there are four families of instruments. The instruments in the brass family have basic similarities (all made of brass), but also basic differences. It takes skill to hear the difference between the various brass instruments (trumpet, trombone, French horn, tuba).

2. Practice listening for the differences between instrument families. Helpful recordings are: "String Quartet No. 3" (Balzac), and

"Sextet For Winds," Op. 71 (Beethoven, *Spectrum of Music,* Bk. 4, rec. 7). Refer also to *The Magic of Music* (Bk. 3, pp. 54–61) and to the *Instruments of the Orchestra* (*RCA Victor,* LE-6000).

3. Sing "Marching to Pretoria," the song of the workers of South African diamond mines (*Making Music Your Own,* Bk. 2, p. 116).

• The Concept of Production

Production: the making of goods, or growing and harvesting of crops.

1. Point out to the children that music can also be seen as production. To do this, we usually perform a composition someone else created. Performing is an important musicianly role. It requires practicing (like growing, if you were a plant), so that eventually the performance (like a crop or flower) is ready.

2. Give the following directions on a job card in your music learning center:

(a) Choose one of the following compositions to perform on the bells, recorder, autoharp, or other classroom instrument:
    "Jingle Bells"
    "Row, Row, Row Your Boat"

(b) Practice your selection until you can perform it smoothly, without stopping or stumbling during the piece.

(c) When you are satisfied that your selection is ready, perform the piece for a friend or your class.

3. Choose one or several of the following songs for a class performance:

"We Are Good Musicians" (German, *New Dimensions in Music,* Bk. 2, p. 134).
"Corn Grinding Song" (Amerindian, *New Dimensions in Music,* Bk. 3, p. 97).
"Life Is Just Fine on the Farm" (*Silver Burdett Music,* Bk. 4, p. 202).
"Erie Canal" (American, *Exploring Music,* Bk. 5, p. 58).

• The Concept of Transportation

Transportation: the movement of goods or people from one place to another.

1. Trains have a fascination for children. Play the recording by Villa Lobos, "Little Train of the Caipira" (*RCA Adventures in Music,*

Gr. 3, Vol. 1), and ask the children to listen to how the composer expresses the starting and stopping of the train.

2. Sing one or several of the following songs about trains:

"Train Is A-Coming" (Spiritual, *Exploring Music,* Bk. 2, p. 101)
"The Daily Express" (Harvey, *Spectrum of Music,* Bk. 3, p. 32)
"Down in the Subway" (Traditional melody, *Spectrum of Music,* Bk. 2, p. 162)

3. Lead the children in a discussion of other modes of transportation. Several songs listed might enhance the concept such as travel by boat or by animals:

"Going Down to Cairo" (American, *Exploring Music,* Bk. 2, p. 95)
"Slumber Boat" (Gaynor, *Exploring Music,* Bk. 2, p. 88)
"Hare Burroquito" (Spanish, *Spectrum of Music,* Bk. 2, p. 88)
"I Ride on Old Paint" (Cowboy, *Spectrum of Music,* Bk. 4, p. 13)

NOTE: Songs can also be found about buses and cars:

"The Bus Song" (American, *New Dimensions in Music,* Bk. 2, p. 26)
"Riding in My Car" (Woody Guthrie, *New Dimensions in Music,* Bk. 2, p. 11)

• **The Concept of Warehouse**

Warehouse: a building in which goods are stored until they are needed.

1. Lead the children in a discussion about our memory as a warehouse. When we listen to a musical composition, it may be a long one. In that case we need to store up the memories of the sounds as we hear them, like the themes, the beat, the tone color used. We will want to take them out again (recall them and recognize them) when they are needed later on in the piece or near the end.

2. Listen to "Miserlou" (Michael Herman, *Happy Folk Dances,* RCA Victor, LPM-1620). Store up in your memory the way the piece begins (the opening theme). See if you can tell when the composer uses it again in his composition. When you recognize themes in folk dances, you can tell when to change dance steps.

3. Learn the Greek dance to "Miserlou." Find a folk dance from a different country, or ask the children to bring in a recording for a dance they can work out with their classmates.

Middle Childhood

Older children possess a growing understanding of man's interdependence, as well as a more developed grasp of geographic principles. Revenue and delta provide two topics for this level.

• The Concept of Revenue

Revenue: income, especially that collected by a government through taxes, for public use.

1. Discuss the concepts inherent in the definition. When the government collects taxes the money is put together into one sum, called revenue, so that it will be available for the good of everyone, the public. The income that produces the revenue grows more and more as each taxpayer contributes his part.

2. Lead the children in a performance in order to demonstrate how income "grows," by adding instrumental sounds to a recording. Many recordings are suitable. One is "Ballad of Bonnie and Clyde" (*Living Marimbas,* RCA Camden, CAS-2253). Follow the steps given below, or put these instructions on job cards for your music learning center.

(a) Choose a conductor who will be the "tax collector."
(b) Begin the recording with no added rhythmic sounds from the class, or small group, no "revenue."
(c) As the tax collector points to each taxpayer, that child adds a sound to the piece and continues playing the sound (vocal, body, environmental, or musical instrument) in a rhythmic pattern or steady beat, to show that his contribution is now in the general revenue, a part of the government's income.
(d) By the end of the piece all the "revenue" should be in. We can hear it all.

3. Play a variation of the above. All instruments begin at once with the recording. The conductor, this time the "mayor" spends the revenue for public works, pointing to each child to remove his sound until the recording is playing alone, and the "revenue" is empty.

4. Discuss the way that composers add sounds to their music after beginning a piece with very few sounds. This has nothing to do with revenue, but you will notice the "growth" or "decline" of musical parts in a composition if you listen to new sounds being added, or sounds that have become familiar, begin to disappear.

5. Listen to the following selections, or others more readily available, and count the number of times the theme is heard.

"Chamber Concerto for Piano, Violin and 13 Wind Instruments" (Berg, Connoisseur, PLPS624)
"Brighter" (*Carole King Music,* ODE-SP77013)
"Symphony No. 1" excerpt, Third Movement (Mahler, Columbia, CSP11613) (The "Frère Jacques" theme is easily discernible, with orchestral buildup.)
"Sabre Dance" (Khachaturian) (The short theme appears frequently, in vigorous surroundings. A quiet, pleasant middle section might seem like "expenditures," and then "collection" resumes.)

• **The Concept of Delta**

Delta: land that is built up at the mouth of a river; the river carries land and soil along as it flows to the sea, and deposits it at the mouth.

1. Discuss the similarities between the accumulation of taxes to form a government's revenue and the accumulation of soil to build up a delta. Music is also a buildup of musical sounds to form a total musical texture. (See the lesson on revenue.)

2. Lead the class in an experience of group composition. "Delta" has interesting possibilities for the subject of a musical composition such as steady, even flow of sound, particles of new timbres (soil) being picked up and carried along, and the climax, when the river reaches the sea and the "soil" is left behind at the delta.

3. Listen to "The Moldau" by Smetana to perceive how he depicts the ending when his river flows out to sea. (*Bowmar,* BOL #60).

4. Sing "Gentle Rivers Run" (*Silver Burdett Music*, Bk. 6, p. 131).

2

Integrating Music with Science

Science has an interdisciplinary nature, for it deals with the biological, physical, and earth science concepts of our environment. In this section, the lesson ideas concentrate mainly on the physical world of sound and energy as these may relate to music. Some scientific terms are used to explore creative ways of thinking about music.

The lesson suggestions encourage the inquiry skills generally associated with scientific processes. These are observing, measuring, describing, comparing, classifying, ranking, collecting, and experimenting. In helping children to organize data and to draw conclusions, the following outline may be useful. Attend to those behaviors in which a child is beginning to develop proficiency as he handles sound phenomena, or develops musical skills.

Observing: Have the children use their ears to perceive, and then describe verbally or through movement what they observe.

Measuring: In early childhood, have the children compare unknowns with a known and familiar standard such as their own voice, a dog's bark, a plane overhead, a truck on the street, and other sounds.

Describing: Have the children show in body movement, verbally, or graphically in line or color, the properties of sound or energy they observed.

Comparing: Help the children learn to sort or group sounds and instruments with respect to their differences and similarities.

Classifying: Provide opportunities for the children to group sounds according to their characteristics. This may include grouping songs, dances, listening selections, as well as creative sound experiments

Ranking: Use opportunities for the children to sort out the important data (relative to sound) from the unimportant data. For instance, words in a song may distract from attention to the movement of the melodic line. Singing on a neutral syllable, or humming, or playing a kazoo removes that verbal distraction.

Experimenting: Have the children practice different ways of expressing a

musical idea, using body sounds, environmental sounds, and available instruments.

In the following you will find ideas for both early childhood and middle childhood in the physical sciences and the earth sciences.

RELATING MUSIC AND THE PHYSICAL SCIENCES

In the physical sciences children study matter and energy, and the interchange of various forms of energy among material things. The ideas in this area include concepts of intensity, frequency, energy, tempo, and duration.

Early Childhood

For young children the approach to music as sound phenomena can be based mainly on the characteristics of sound. The children should focus their efforts around the elements of music and sound in their environment in terms of describing (through motion, graphics, or verbalization), comparing, and ranking information about the characteristics of pitch, duration, timbre, and dynamics.

- **Categorizing Intensity**

1. In each of four boxes display five or six sound sources varied enough to provide at least three timbre categories such as metallic, wood, and randomly mixed according to naturally louder and softer sounds.
2. Divide the class into four groups, one for each box. Instruct the children to line up the instruments in front of the box in the following sequence: loudest to the left, softest to the right. Children determine their decisions by shaking, blowing, striking, or plucking each item. They may work in groups or singly depending upon the learning setting.
3. Encourage discussions in which the children will engage as differences in opinion arise from the use of more or less energy in activating the sounds. The process here is more important than complete agreement on a correct lineup.

- **Comparing Intensity**

1. Provide four empty boxes labelled: *very loud, loud, soft, very*

soft, and display the same instruments as those listed in the previous lesson (or a similar grouping).

2. Instruct the children to classify the sounds and place them in the boxes so that the loudest sounds are in one group and the softest in another. Much discussion will ensue from their attempts to classify the two middle groups into "not quite as loud" and "not quite as soft."

3. Point out the differences in dynamics when more or less energy is expended to produce the sound, i.e., the stronger the force employed (blowing, striking), the louder the sound.

- **Categorizing Pitches (Intensity)**

1. Display three or four metallic environmental sound sources such as safe kitchen or work utensils, pans, and a heavy metal spoon for striking. Place them in your Music Center.

By means of a cassette, instruct the child to arrange the lowest sound on the left, the highest sound on the right (thus imitating a keyboard or tone bell arrangement to be met in later musical experiences).

2. On another cassette for another time, give instructions to classify the sounds according to how *long* they last.

NOTE: You may wish to correlate the preceding with a nature lesson and limit the sound sources to those from nature. Ideas: paper bag of dry leaves, can of rocks, twigs and water in a container to be blown by using a hollow reed.

- **Controlling Energy and Speed (Game Corner)**

1. Provide a variety of any or all of the following instruments: car parts (old brake drums and shock absorbers), homemade drums and shakers, manufactured classroom instruments, classroom environmental sounds.

Direct the children to work with partners, using the following instructions on task cards (or cassettes):

(a) Make up a pattern of three sounds, two loud and one soft, in an order chosen from these possibilities:

L L S
L S L
S L L

(b) Ask your partner to imitate your pattern. If your partner succeeds, it is his turn to make up a pattern.

NOTE: On other cards, increase the sounds to four, then to five, making up new loud/soft patterns for possible choices.

2. At another time, help the children control how long a sound lasts. Have L = long, and S = short, and use the game plan above.

- **Exploring Dynamics (Game Corner)**

Make four charts (Fig. 4). Use *f* for loud and *p* for soft. Divide the class into four groups. Provide several different instruments for each group.

Children take turns as follows:

(1) Choose an instrument.
(2) Briefly perform on the instrument your "own thing," as directed by #1, then #2, #3, and #4, down the chart. The group evaluates each performer for accuracy in following the loud and soft symbols.
(3) When all have finished their turn, rotate to the next chart.

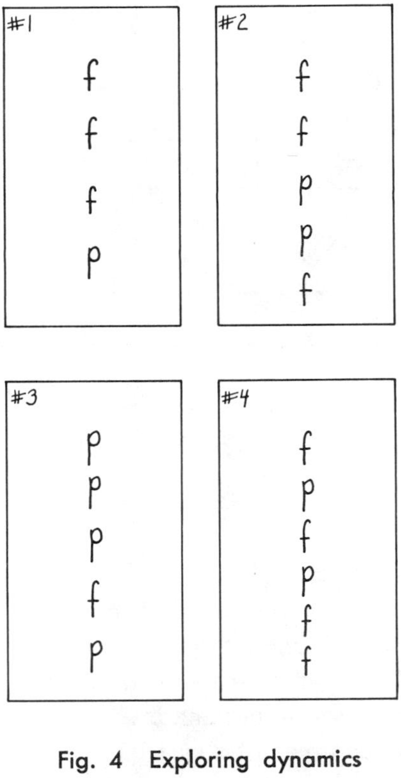

Fig. 4 Exploring dynamics

When all have played all charts, children trade instruments and begin again.

• **Exploring Duration (Game Corner)**

Display instruments that sustain sound such as the triangle, gong, jingle bells, and guiro (if the children can control the speed of the stroke across the ribs).

Prepare charts as for "Exploring Dynamics," but with varying long and short horizontal lines, as shown in Fig. 5.

Show the children how to stop a triangle or pan from continuing to ring by grasping it while it vibrates.

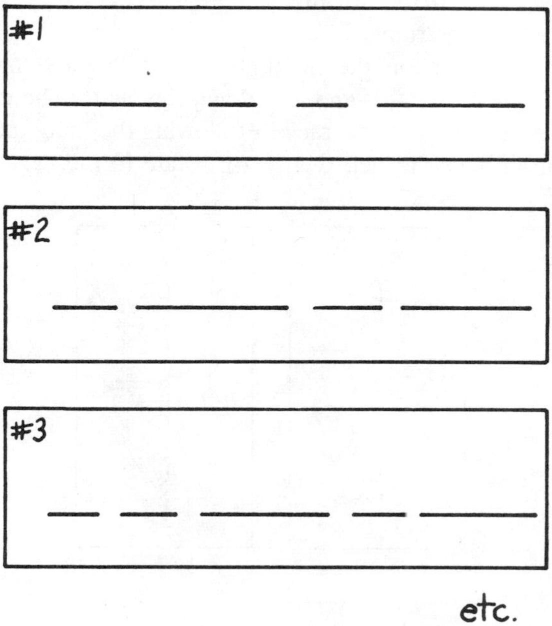

Fig. 5 Exploring duration

Middle Childhood

For children at the middle level of elementary school, place the emphasis on relationship and utilization, that is, on the use and value aspects of sound and music materials.

Sound and silence separate segments of time. Have the child at this age experiment with sound materials, exploring time spans in much the same way as areas of space have been explored in science studies.

The physical sciences deal with energy and changes that take place in the environment. Two topics easily relating to music are those of distortion and pollution.

• **Exploring Invariants and Distortion**

1. Lead the class in a discussion of the scientific notion of distortion. How can a sound be changed, or distorted, without altering it entirely? It can be changed in many ways without everything about it being changed. The properties that do not change are called "invariants." A "variant" is a thing that changes. In music we can keep the timbre the same and vary the pitch; keep the pitch the same and vary the dynamics.

2. Play two different versions of the English folk melody "Greensleeves." (One source may be found in *Silver Burdett Music,* Bk. 5, p. 143). Notice the melody as the invariant. List the variables that change such as the timbre, the harmony, the texture.

NOTE: The lists will depend upon versions used. Encourage children to bring recordings from home to lend variety to the versions heard in class.

3. Listen to Olivia Newton-John's rendition of "The River's Too Wide" (MCA-411). Ask the children to design a call chart showing the sequence of variation in accompaniments to this brief melody.

4. At another time, do the above with Cat Stevens's "Morning Has Broken" (A&M, SP4313). Notice especially the modulation, or change of key, in the third verse. This alters the melody by creating a heightened sense of tension, raising the entire melody slightly, but not altering any other feature.

• **The Concept of Pollution**

Pollution: the unclean condition of the earth's soil, air, and water when waste materials are poured into them.

1. Lead the class in a discussion with the question, "Is there a way to portray 'uncleanness' through music?" What might you use if you were the composer? Why would you make your choice of sounds?

2. Put the following instructions on task cards or a cassette in the music or science center:

(a) Make up a composition entitled "Pollution."

(b) Decide on one of the three natural resources as the subject of your composition—soil, air, or water.

(c) Choose an instrument or sound source to portray that sound source in its "pure" form. Decide on the sounds you will use to represent pollution using one, two, or three different "pollutors."

(d) Begin your piece with the "pure resource." Introduce "pollution" either all at once or gradually.

(e) Decide on the ending of your composition. If you begin with purity and end with pollution, this would be like AB form in music. If you begin and end with purity, that would be like ABA form. Is there any other musical form you could use?

(f) Play your composition for the class or record it.

3. As a class or group project, compose the above in rondo form. Precede the activity with some class research on water pollution. Have there been other times in history when people have had trouble with impurities in their water supply? What polluted their water? How did they purify their water? Are their troubles with the problem over now? Rondo form looks like this: A B A C A. The first part returns between two dissimilar parts.

4. Listen to "Variations on a Theme of Satie" by Blood, Sweat and Tears (*New Dimensions in Music,* Bk. 6, Rec. 9). Is this version of Satie's theme an example of something pure, like water, soil, or air, getting filled with waste materials?

5. At another time, listen to programmatic music that portrays today's pollution problems such as "Steel Foundry" (Mossolov, *Sounds of New Music,* Folkways, FX6160).

RELATING MUSIC AND THE EARTH SCIENCES

This aspect of science deals with air, water, atmosphere, life on the planet, and its preservation. No direct relationship to music is presented in terms of sound-producing phenomena here, but rather, the imaginative use of scientific terminology has provided topics for lesson ideas.

Early Childhood

Topics explored for this level include satellites and evaporation. Many similar concepts will occur to you and to the children when your imaginations get involved.

• **The Concept of Satellite**

Satellite: a smaller body that revolves around a larger body.

1. Lead the children in the following discussion: An ostinato in music behaves somewhat like a satellite—it revolves around a theme that has the greater prominence and importance. An ostinato in music does not usually stand alone, nor do satellites. A satellite needs something around which to revolve.

2. Play the recording "The Snow Is Dancing" by Debussy, from *Children's Corner Suite* (*RCA Adventures in Music,* Gr. 3, Vol. 1), without giving the children the title. Ask them to listen for the background rhythmic ostinato prevalent throughout much of the selection (16th note patterns). Because of the rapid note values, a sense of movement and "revolving" may be discovered by the children.

Ask them to move by tiptoeing to the 16th note pattern, , in large circles, as a satellite in space. Choose a large object (table or the like) as the "Earth" around which to "revolve."

3. Listen to "Children's Dance" from Hanson's *Merry Mount Suite* (*RCA Adventures in Music,* Gr. 3, Vol. 1). Discover the two rhythmic patterns:

(a) 

(b) 

Divide the class into two groups, one for each of the above patterns. Clap the pattern with the recording, each group separately (to establish independence).

Add rhythm instruments to the clapping. Each pattern becomes a rhythmic ostinato played throughout the selection. The ostinato can become like a "satellite," moving with the music, but subordinate to it. Playing along with the complete piece is like "one revolution" around the "larger body."

• **The Concept of Evaporation**

Evaporate: to pass off, or disappear, in the form of vapor.

1. Compare a musical composition to a puddle of water. When

the puddle begins to evaporate, it diminishes, for there is less water present. A composer can diminish the sound in his music by writing fewer and fewer notes to be played by the performers, or by calling for fewer instruments. This causes less sound. Composers sometimes do this near the ending of a piece.

2. Listen to Offenbach's "Barcarolle" (*RCA Adventures in Music,* Gr. 3, Vol. 1). Help the children notice how the composer creates a "fading" impression at the end of the piece.

3. Encourage the children to bring recorded examples of music that fades, or "evaporates" at the end. Try to discover when the composer wrote the parts to fade, and when the effect is done by the engineer in the recording studio. The latter is understood if the children behave as the engineer by turning down the volume dial on the record player, creating their own "evaporation" control.

4. Make two lists of fading music, one done by the composer, the other by the recording engineer. Below is a beginning:

composer—"The Snow Is Dancing" (Debussy); "Dripsody" (LeCaine, *New Dimensions in Music,* EC, 6)
engineer—"In the Beginning" (Aretha Franklin, Columbia, GT-31355); "The River's Too Wide" (Olivia Newton-John, MCA-411)

Middle Childhood

Renewable and nonrenewable resources of the earth have been receiving much attention in science classes in recent years. Two concepts related to man's concern for his environment give rise to the following lesson ideas on conservation and filters. Think of other topics the children would enjoy pursuing through musical activities.

• The Concept of Conservation

Conservation: taking care of natural resources so they will not be spoiled or wasted, but will be used wisely.

1. Encourage the children to discuss silence as a resource that needs to be protected. Some sound put into silence can be lovely, just as some odors or colors put into air can be lovely. But the pure air or the pure silence (relatively speaking) should predominate. They are limited natural resources, while man's designs or demands upon them

can be unlimited. Silence is the opposite of sound. If we fill all silence with sound (sound in every place—sound all the time), we will have *used up* all the silence we have. We try to conserve silence because it is precious to us. Why? So far, our government has very few laws to ensure the proper use of our natural resource, silence. In the future, government leadership and planning along with public cooperation will protect its use.

2. Listen to the way composers use silence in their compositions. It adds variety to the sounds they plan. Examples: "Pas de Caractere" from *Sleeping Beauty Ballet Suite,* Tchaikowsky; "Ein Feste Burg," Bach; "Largo: Allegro Vivace," Haydn, Symphony #102, First Movement. (All three may be found in *New Dimensions in Music,* Bk. 6, Rec. 8.)

3. Ask the children to bring a recording to play for the class that demonstrates silence used in music.

• The Concept of Filter

Filter: something that is used to strain liquid or air. Filters can take dirt out of smoke or water.

1. Explain to the class that before the use of electronics, composers did their own "music filtering" by discontinuing certain parts in the composition. This does not mean that filtering took out unwanted sounds, as filters remove unwanted dirt in our natural environment. But the similarity is present when we understand that a composer removes a theme, or a section of the orchestra, by not assigning a part for that musical element.

2. Listen to "Farondole" by Bizet (*RCA Adventures in Music,* Gr. 6, Vol 1). In the opening section, the entire orchestra is heard playing the theme, then only the string section, while the rest of the orchestra is silent, "filtered out." Another example is "Contradance" from *Divertimento No. 8* (Mozart, *Exploring Music,* Bk. 2, Rec. 7).

3. Today, sounds can be filtered out of recordings electronically. Ask the children to bring an example of such a recording to class. If you live in or near a large city, visit a recording studio to see the control panel that the sound engineer uses to mix and filter sounds being recorded from several microphones onto a multitrack tape.

3

Integrating Music with Mathematics

Mathematics deals with concepts of quantity and space, and their relationships. In this section, the mathematical approaches to relationships are explored as these may be related to music. The ability to perceive and analyze patterns is of great importance in the modern approach to mathematics. Consequently, children are led to discover rules and patterns for themselves.

Patterns are also important in music. Music is the expressive use of sound patterns. Making up sound patterns and listening carefully to patterns composed by others will help develop the child's perception of music, as well as strengthen his understanding of relationships in general.

In the following game and lesson suggestions, attention has been given to concepts of like and different, counting, sets, sequencing, patterns, and relationships. The first group of ideas is directed to young children, while the later ideas presuppose greater maturity.

Early Childhood

Encourage children to recognize instrumental sounds (timbres) by sound as well as by sight, for music is an aural art.

• Exploring Like and Different in a Game Center

Categorizing Game

Provide sets of classroom instruments: several shakers, rhythm sticks, wood blocks, bolts, tambourines, and the like.

Have a container for each set (shoe box or canned good carton) with a picture of that instrument pasted or drawn on the side of the container.

Display the instruments, in a mixture, on the floor or low table in front of the boxes. Direct the children to sound or play each instru-

ment, and then put it into the appropriate box. When all the instruments are boxed, the children count those in each container and report to the teacher for an evaluation. This activity may be done by an individual child, or by small groups, who may then check each other's decisions.

Classifying in Sets Game

1. Gather together several of each of the following: homemade instruments, manufactured rhythm instruments, safe kitchen utensils, other environmental sound sources (keys that rattle on a ring, rulers that can be struck together, and so on).

Discuss with the children the differences between things we make, those we buy, sound-makers from the kitchen, and other things.

Label four cartons with a symbol readily associated with each category, and place two pairs of instruments in each box. Direct the child to take all the instruments from a box of his choice and place them in a row in front of the box. Count the number of instruments. Play each one. When two are alike, place them together, next to each other. Point out the sets of twos when you evaluate the child's completed task.

2. At another time, mix the instruments in the cartons to provide combinations of two alike and one different; three alike and two different. Count the instruments that are alike. Arrange like instruments into sets.

Make up a musical piece with the sounds.

Associating Game

1. Place two different types of instruments at a time in front of the child. Play another instrument that is the same as one or the other displayed. Given the two choices, ask the child to answer you by playing the same instruments as yours.

2. At another time, add three instruments to choose from, then four, then five. (The teacher must always have an identical instrument to match each of the choices presented to the child.)

3. Ask the child to name the instrument, to recognize it by sight, and eventually to recognize it by sound (with eyes closed, or back turned). The preceding games may be done with one child, small groups, or the class, depending upon the learning setting.

Sequencing Game

1. Arrange the following (or similar) rhythm instruments in a half-circle on the floor: shaker, tambourine, pair of rhythm sticks, drum, triangle, and tone block. Have the children sit in a group in such a way that all can see the instruments.

Ask one child to play one of the instruments, and then choose another child to copy him. The first child acts as the evaluator of the imitation. If the second child succeeds, he does "his thing" on the instrument of his choice, and chooses an imitator. If the second child fails, another child attempts to imitate adequately, while he drops out of the game. The game continues until all have succeeded, or, if the playing becomes challenging enough, until a winner emerges.

2. At another time, the performer may play "his own thing" on each instrument, and then either repeat these in the same order, or choose another child to attempt to copy him in the proper order.

NOTE: This game and variations of the preceding games are also suitable for retarded or handicapped children. A child in a wheelchair may play instruments identical to those on the floor, but within his reach (on his lap or a table top).

- **Counting**

Numerical Order Game

Have the children informally scattered in the room, then play the recording "Tinker Tinker Doo" (H. Glass, *Activities for Individualization in Movement and Music,* Educational Activities, Inc.). Ask them to act out the directions of the song: moving one arm, then two arms; both arms and head; arms, head, and one shoulder; arms, head, and shoulders; add one foot; add both feet.

Sequential Patterning Game

Follow similar directions, as above, to any of the following songs:

"This Old Man"
"Ten Little Indians"
"Counting Song" (*Growing with Music,* Bk. 2)
"Counting Stars" and "One, Two, Three" (*New Dimensions in Music,* Bk. 2)
"Johnny Works with One Hammer" (Burnett, *Melody, Movement and Language*)

Songs for Counting

The following songs will enhance programs where repetition is made enjoyable through song:

"Honey, You Can't Love One" (Traditional, *Exploring Music,* Bk. 2, p. 110)
"Noah's Ark" (American, *Discovering Music Together,* Bk. 4, p. 117)
"Bye 'n Bye" (Texan folk game, *New Dimensions in Music,* Bk. 2, p. 56)
"The Angel Band" (American, *New Dimensions in Music,* Bk. 2, p. 6)
"Ten in a Bed" (Traditional, *New Dimensions in Music,* Bk. 2, p. 163)

Counting and Performing, Left to Right

1. Divide your set of resonator bells, at random, into five subsets of four bells each. Line up each subset with the longest bell on the left (lowest sound) and the shortest bell on the right (highest sound).

Divide the class into five groups, with one mallet for each group. Provide each group with a task card with instructions similar to those in the sample cards shown in Fig. 6.

Group I

2 strikes on the first bell
4 strikes on the second bell
5 strikes on the fourth bell

Group II

2 strikes on the second bell
4 strikes on the third bell
6 strikes on the fourth bell

Group III

1 strike on the first bell
2 strikes on the second bell
3 strikes on the third bell
4 strikes on the fourth bell

Group IV

4 strikes on the first bell
4 strikes on the second bell
5 strikes on the third bell

Group V

3 strikes on the first bell
4 strikes on the third bell
5 strikes on the fourth bell

Fig. 6 Sample task cards

Each group reads and performs its task, one child after another. After the performance of all in the group, children move to the next set of bells and the new task card.

2. At another time, stay at the same set of bells but play a different task card. Again, move to a new set of bells, with the same group task card at each new set of bells. Later, the children can select numerals from a deck of cards or write up their own original list of numerals on the board to follow.

3. After some experience, have children select four or five bells and compose a musical selection that follows a specific number system they devise. Encourage an evaluation of their piece and possible revisions for more desirable effects.

• Learning About Meter Through Sets

Task 1—Triple Meter

1. Discuss with the children the division of musical beats into duple meter (sets of twos) and triple meter (sets of threes). We can tell which meter is used when listening to music if we listen for the accent or strong pulse. Follow these steps:

(a) Listen to the recording of "Music" by Carole King (ODE, SP-77013). Tap gently the steady pulse. (It moves along quite rapidly so your tapping should not be slow.)
(b) Notice that one pulse seems stronger; tap it heavier, the others lighter. The pattern, or set, turns out to be strong, weak, weak, or S w w, S w w.

2. Try other examples of recorded music found in many collections. Suggestions:

"Minuetto" from *Divertimento No. 2* (Mozart, *Discovering Music Together*)
"The Sleigh Ride" from *German Dances* (Mozart, *New Dimensions in Music,* Bk. 4, Rec. 8)
"Fantasia on Greensleeves" (Williams, *New Dimensions in Music,* Bk. 4, Rec. 8)

Task 2—Duple Meter

1. Ask the children to discover what meter Simon and Garfunkel use to portray the feeling of walking in "Feeling Groovy" ("59th Street

Bridge Song," *Parsley, Sage, Rosemary and Thyme,* Columbia, CS-9363). Tap along steadily. Notice that one tap feels stronger than the other—Strong-weak, Strong-weak, or S w, S w. If *one* weak beat appears between each strong beat, we call the combination "duple meter."

On paper, or on the chalkboard, make strokes in time to the music, tall strokes for strong beats, short strokes for weak beats: ┃ ╻ ┃ ╻ (If *two* weak beats appear between each strong one, we call that combination triple meter: ┃ ╻ ╻ ┃ ╻ ╻.)

2. Play one of the following selections or similar ones in duple meter:

"On the Street Where You Live" from *My Fair Lady* (*New Dimensions in Music,* Bk. 4, Rec. 7)
"Fiddler on the Roof" (*New Dimensions in Music,* Bk. 4, Rec. 7)

Middle Childhood

In mathematics for the eight- to eleven-year-old child, a relationship can be drawn by looking at the parameters of both mathematics and music: mathematics deals with *space;* music exists in *time.* Both can be said to be quantitative. Put in another way, the elements of music are put together and can be thought of as a sum or combination of sounds. However, these sounds appear over a span of time rather than being perceived in a given space.

• Comparing Mathematics with Music

Lead the children in a discussion of the following comparisons:

Mathematics	*Music*
A number is an idea.	A pitch is an idea.
A number may be written by using a symbol called a numeral.	A pitch may be written by using a symbol called a note.
A time line is used to illustrate graphically the relative position of numbers.	A staff is used to illustrate graphically the relative position of pitches.

Mathematics is governed by basic principles such as the commutative principles of addition and multiplication:

a, b, and c are any numbers.

$a + b = b + a$

$a \times b = b \times a$

The ordering of the above elements, i.e., which is first or last, does not matter in many spatial considerations.

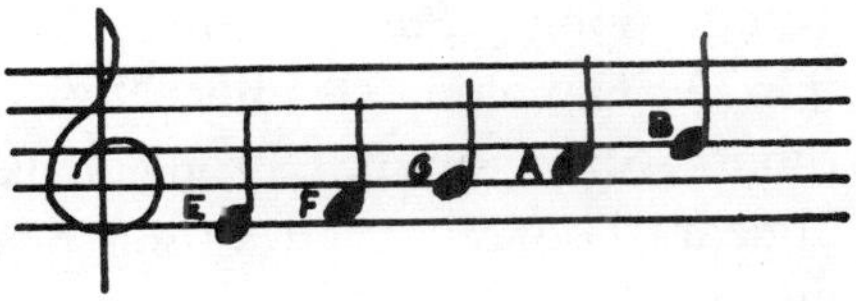

Music helps us to understand our temporal world. It is not governed by the same principles as those of the spatial world. For instance:

a, b, and c are any sounds.

$a + b \neq b + a$

In music, if you add one sound before another, a different effect may be created. The ordering of musical elements, i.e., which is first or last, is important in music.

- **Perceiving Sound Organization**

Listen to the recording, "Good News" (*Discovering Music Together,* SL900). List the sounds in the order that you hear them appear. Ask the children to tell what is first, what is last. Here is a list of the sounds:

(1) bells
(2) wood block
(3) piano
(4) voice

This is the order in which they appear:

1 and 2
1, 2, and 3
1, 2, 3, and 4
3 alone
1, 2, and 3
3 alone
1 and 2

2. At another time, listen to "Poor Wayfaring Stranger" (recording noted above). Notice that the guitar plays alone, then the voice enters. How does it end?

3. Compare "Cherry Blooms" ("Sakura") as recorded differently in several of the various music series books such as *Making Music Your Own,* Bk. 4, and *New Dimensions in Music,* Bk. 6. In *Discovering Music Together,* Bk. 4, the instruments appear in the following order:

(1) gong
(2) chimes
(3) koto
(4) chimes, chorus, cello, flute
(5) all above, plus soprano voice
(6) gong, koto, chimes
(7) flute and chimes
(8) gong

• **Using Repetitions to Create Designs**

1. Divide the class into two or three groups. Appoint timekeepers or have each group choose one. Give the following directions:

(a) Each group will create a soundpiece.
(b) The piece will last one minute.
(c) The sounds used will be in three sets:
  (1) metallic sounds found in the room
  (2) vocal sounds without words
  (3) handclapping
(d) Alternate plans of action for procedure:
  —all sounds begin together
  —sound (1) begins before (2) and (3)
or —sound (2) begins before (1) and (3)
or —sound (3) begins before (1) and (2).

Direct the children to discuss other possible variations. Is any particular way the correct one? Note with the children that music is not governed by the same laws or rules that may govern mathematics, so choices can be left to the composer.

2. Perform the compositions for the other groups and discuss the designs or patterns noticed in each.

• **Associating Design in Music**

Experience 1

Place the following pattern on the chalkboard:

Have the class clap the pattern while foot-tapping a steady beat, (♩ = 1 steady beat; clap for each ♩ ; 𝄽 = 1 steady beat; wait for each rest.)

Assign one student or ask a volunteer to play the following resonator bells in this rhythmic pattern:

Listen to Cat Stevens's "Peace Train" (*Teaser and the Firecat,* A&M, SP4313). Ask the children to listen for their pattern. Does it ever change? Play the pattern along with the recording.

Experience 2

In a music center have the following directions on task cards, with a set of resonator bells:

Task cards

> 1. Place the following three resonator bells in front of you:
>
> C#, E, F#.
>
> Play alternately and slowly
>
> E and F#, 8 times.
>
> We will call this PART I.

> 2. Repeat what you played on Task card 1, that is:
>
> E and F#, 8 times,
>
> slowly and alternately.
>
> We will call this PART II.

3. Now play, alternately and slowly

E and C#, 8 times.

We will call this PART III.

Now repeat PART I. This will become PART IV.

4. The entire pattern looks like this:

PART I:	E—F#	8 times
PART II:	E—F#	8 times
PART III:	E—C#	8 times
PART IV:	E—F#	8 times

5. Now listen to "Home Again" by Carole King (*Carole King Tapestry*, ODE, SP77009).

Play your pattern in steady beats along with the recording. (PART III begins with the words, "Snow is cold . . .").

Can you hear when to return to the E—F# set? After some practice you will probably stop counting the 8 times, for you will hear when to change your pattern.

- **Predicting Final Numbers from Following a Pattern of Numbers**

In a music center provide the following: an autoharp; cards with numbers in a sequential pattern, with the final number a blank ——, to be supplied by the child as he perceives the pattern in the preceding sequence.

Assign two chords to be played alternately on the autoharp such as F and C_7. Direct the child to play the number of strokes designated on the card, alternating chords for each new numeral.

Example: Chords:	F	C_7	F	C_7	F
Sequential Pattern:	2	4	6	8	?

Suggestions for task cards:

(a) *Chords:*	F	C_7	F	C_7	F
Sequential Pattern:	3	4	5	6	?

(b) *Chords:*	Dmin	A_7	Dmin	A_7	Dmin
Sequential Pattern:	11	10	8	5	?

(c) *Three Chords:*	C	F	G_7	F	G_7	C
Sequential Pattern:	1	3	2	4	3	?

4

Integrating Music with Language Arts

Music experiences can provide imaginative activities that will sharpen the child's perception of aural comprehension and communication, as well as increase his understanding and enjoyment of both oral language and musical expression. The following ideas provide opportunities for children to listen for specific information, for the main ideas in song stories and programmatic music, for understanding both word and sound relationships, and for the evaluation of meanings of words and sounds heard.

LEARNING TO LISTEN

Listening is one of the most important musical behaviors that we try to develop in children in order to assist in the full enjoyment of the musical world opening up to them. Listening is also an important skill in the development of language. In fostering the growth of this skill, remember that listening is more than just hearing. It really means giving active and conscious attention to the sounds we hear in order to grasp the meaning these convey.

Early Childhood

Many examples are found of giving young children simple directions to follow. Success in dealing with language depends upon the child's ability to grasp the meaning of the directions and to act upon that knowledge. The following lesson and game ideas demand listening for specific information, for main ideas, for relationships and evaluations among sounds and words. Musical concepts and activities provide the experiential focus.

• **Listening for Specific Information**

Help the children listen for numerical order, for sequence, for descriptive terms, and for recognition of pitch concepts. They may respond through moving, performing, and describing verbally, thereby increasing their ability to use their language skills more adequately.

Sound Cues

1. Direct the children to find a standing place in the room. Invite one of the class to act as the leader, playing alternately one of the following instruments:

- the shortest resonator bell (high sound)
- the longest resonator bell (low sound)
- a pair of sticks, a tambourine, and a maraca (nonpitched sounds)

Have the leader play the instruments in a corner with his back to the class to avoid giving away "visual cues."

Instruct the children to stand on tiptoe if the high pitch is played, to squat if the low pitch is played, and to remain still if any nonpitched instrument is played. Anyone who misses goes to his seat. The last to remain standing becomes the new leader.

2. At another time, have the leader make a high vocal sound, a low vocal sound, and a number of nonpitched "mouth sounds" such as tongue-clicking, lip-smacking, or blowing, hissing, etc.

Numerical Order Game

Play a series of tones on the resonator bells, singing or saying the name of each as you play. Ask the children to identify a particular one. For example:

- Listen for the name of the *second* tone played.
- Listen for the name of the *lowest* tone played.

Sequence Game 1

Use musical items other than tones on the resonator bells. Line up several different classroom rhythm instruments and play one after another, scrambling the order visually (or have the children close their eyes). Ask the children which instrument you played *third*. A volunteer names the instrument (if he knows the label), or comes up and plays the one he thinks was third.

Sequence Game 2

Display five or six classroom musical instruments on a table or shelf. Give the class simple directions for activities involving three things to do. For example:

- Play the tambourine twice, the drum twice, and the cowbell twice. (Omit at least two other possible instruments displayed, but not called for in the directions.)
- While one child is performing, have the others check his performance against the given directions. Repeat the activity, occasionally having the successful children perform the directions in reverse.

Descriptive Terms Game

Ask one child to describe the sounds made by one of his favorite musical instruments commonly used in the class. (The instruments may be concealed and may include car parts, commercially manufactured or homemade instruments.) The other children close their eyes and listen for the descriptive details in an effort to guess what the instrument is. If no one guesses after the speaker has exhausted his verbal descriptions, invite the listeners to ask questions that can be answered by "Yes" or "No." The child who first correctly identifies the concealed instrument wins the opportunity to replace the speaker.

- **Listening for the Main Idea**

Language arts teachers sometimes read a poem or brief story and then ask the children to give the reading a title. This shows the child's understanding of the main idea in the reading. The same may be done with music. Here are some ideas to try.

The Circus Song

1. Sing the well-known "Circus Song" (Fig. 7). Ask the children to suggest a title for the song that fits the main idea of the text. Make a list of the suggested titles. Have the children evaluate each title, choose one, and then tell them the real title of the song, "The Man on the Flying Trapeze" (Traditional).

2. Other songs to use are:

"Fiddler on the Roof" and "The Shoemaker" (*Growing with Music,* Bk. 2)
"Barnyard Song" (*Exploring Music,* Bk. 2)

Fig. 7 "The Circus Song"

Job Description

Invite a check-out clerk or a letter carrier into the classroom to tell the children about his or her job. After the visit, discuss what this person's job is.

- Using a familiar tune "Three Blind Mice," "Twinkle Twinkle Little Star," "Did You Ever See a Lassie?", make up words to describe this person at work.
- Have the children make up an appropriate title for their song that captures the main focus of the content.

- **Understanding Relationships**

Words are related in various ways. One way may be descriptive, another sequential. For instance, certain words are used to describe the movement of animals or machines. Or, words may appear in songs in specific sequence. Listening for and remembering these relationships are valuable skills. Try the following musical activities to help develop these skills.

Animal Movements

Make word cards showing pictures of animals, their names, and how they move. Have each child choose a card and then a classroom instrument to play that will show how his animal moves.

Have the children take turns playing their instrument to depict the movement of the animal. When the class guesses the animal, the teacher writes the two words on the board. For example:

bird	— flies	frog	— leaps
turtle	— crawls	alligator	— glides
pony	— gallops	rabbit	— hops
worm	— wiggles	squirrel	— climbs
fish	— swims	mouse	— scurries

Sound Description

Every sound we hear is made by something moving. Ask the children to listen for sounds both in and out of school, then plan a class discussion. Talk about where the sounds the children report come from. Use descriptive words that tell how the sound was made, i.e., what kind of motion was used. Also, use words that tell about the sound itself.

Music Center

1. Arrange various classroom instruments in a box or on a table top or shelf.

Prepare six cards each with a large letter, A to F, on the front of each card. On the back of each card write a word describing a kind of motion such as:

A — quick
B — slow
C — smooth
D — jerky
E — fast
F — quiet
} (motion)

Prepare a cassette with the following directions:

(a) Choose an instrument from the box.

(b) Put the cards in a stack in alphabetical order, with the letters face up. Turn the top card over.
(c) Play the instrument as directed by the word on the card. Turn off the cassette while you play.
(d) Turn over each card and do the same until you have played your instrument in all six ways. The next time you come to the center, choose a different instrument to play with the cards.

NOTE: For nonreaders, say each word on the cassette to assist with word recognition on the card.

2. For another set of cards use descriptive words such as: soft, heavy, loud, low, high, deep, gentle, faint, rough. Direct the children to use their voices for the instrument.

Word Sequences

Sing or play a recording of one of the songs listed below, each of which tells a story. Without repeating the song, show the children a jumbled series of illustrations that depict scenes, characters, or events in the song.

"The Animal Fair" (*Exploring Music,* Bk. 2, p. 16). Needed pictures: baboon, monkey, elephant.
"The Cricket's Song" (*Silver Burdett Music,* Bk. 1, p. 46). Needed pictures: treetop, wind, rocks, musical notes.
"C Is for Clouds" (*New Dimensions in Music,* Bk. 2, p. 22). Needed pictures: thunder clouds, lightning, trees blowing, rain on the window pane, sun.

Ask the children to arrange the pictures in their proper order to match the sequence in the song. Repeat the song to check on sequence memory.

Family Characteristics Among Musical Instruments

1. Say aloud a group of musical instrument names in which one of the words does not belong, for example: guitar, banjo, bass fiddle, cello, electric piano.

Ask the children to select the word that does not belong. "Electric piano" is the answer if used in the sense of not being a stringed instrument. Cello might be a valid choice in that it is not usually used in folk or rock music, while all others in the list are. Have the children

talk about the different ways in which musical instruments can be related to each other.

2. Another group of names could be the following: piccolo, violin, trumpet, flute, tuba. Presumably, "violin" is the answer because it is the only instrument not played by blowing into it. Or tuba could be the answer, for it is the only instrument that is very large or plays very low. Help the children recognize in what situations the instruments would be used in varying relationships.

• **Evaluating Sounds and Words**

The manner in which a word is spoken often changes the meaning of the word. Children will gain skill in evaluating expressive meanings if they make up words and tunes to explore the expressive possibilities.

Creative Songs

Separate the resonator bells into three groups, as shown in Fig. 8.

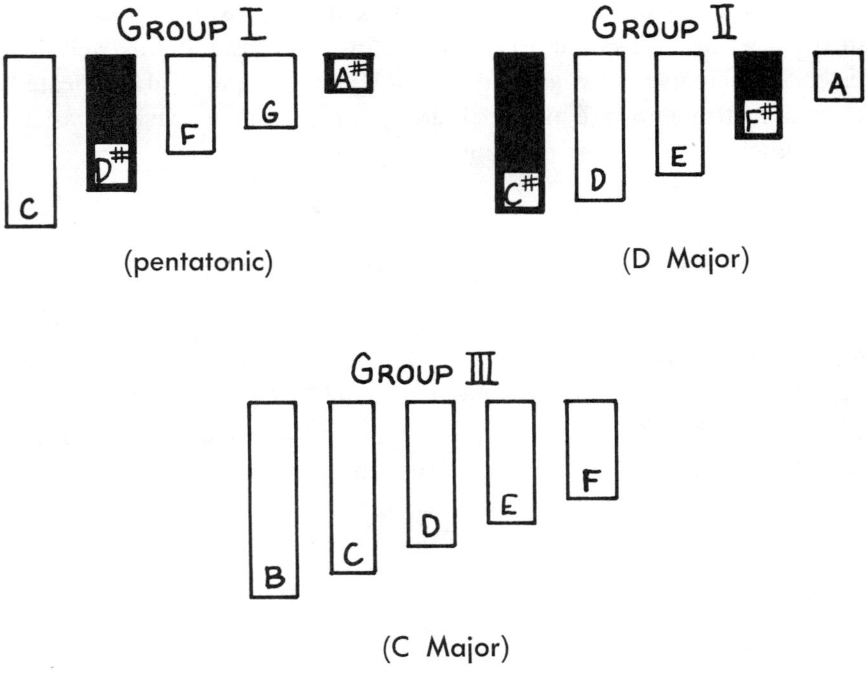

Fig. 8 Groups of resonator bells

Divide the class into three groups, one for each set of bells. Direct the children to make up short statements to sing to a tune they make up with the help of the bells.

Have one child begin the game by singing his tune with three different attitudes. The child who guesses the attitudes that the performer tried to express is the next to get a turn.

Possible attitudes:	*Suggested statements to get started:*
excited	"It's raining outside."
mysterious	"Mary has a pet snake."
disappointed	"The door is locked."
relieved	
frightened	
laughingly	
matter-of-fact	
etc.	

EXPANDING LISTENING SKILLS

More challenge in verbal listening skills is possible with children in the intermediate grades. This is true in music listening as well. We listen to perceive how a song is made longer, parts are repeated, certain instruments are played louder, some themes are emphasized over others, and similar concepts.

Middle Childhood

Older children enjoy changing and rearranging the structure, form, or parts within a musical composition or song to make it more useful, functional, esthetic, or just personal. The following lesson suggestions give an opportunity to be creative, as well as to follow written and oral directions, to remember sequence, to listen for main ideas and for sound sources and their meanings.

• Following Verbal Directions, Aural and Written

Original Compositions

Provide for the performance of original class musical compositions by following the "composer's" verbal directions.

Have the children prepare written directions in advance for a sound improvisation that would express travelling from one city to another by land, or sea, or air.

Have the class listen carefully as one child reads his directions. These may go something like this:

- Play the egg beater to "rev-up" the engine of a car, for starting the trip.
- Shake the maracas loudly at first and then softer and faster as the car picks up speed out of town.
- Turn on the "radio" by beginning to whistle a tune while maracas continue to shake.
- End a trip with a fast roll on the drum, slowing down to a final thud.

Choose a volunteer to perform the soundpiece as he has just heard it described. If he is successful, he then reads the directions he has prepared, and so the game continues.

Harmonizing with Instruments

1. Plan autoharp performances by the children through written directions for chord changes.

2. Instruct the children in and have them practice playing and changing chords smoothly on the autoharp or other harmony instrument such as the ukelele or guitar.

3. Provide the class with heritage or folksong sheets that use a few chords in specific sequences. On cards, prepare written directions to be followed in order to accompany the song. For example, "Down in the Valley":

(a) During the first line of the song, play the F chord, except at the last word, when you change to C_7.
(b) On the second line, continue the C_7 chord, except for the last word, when you change back to F.
(c) Third line, same as the first.
(d) Fourth line, same as the second.

Below are the words of the song. The chords have been given here for the benefit of the teacher and should not appear on the song sheet used by the child. Instead, he should either listen for the directions read to him, or read and follow the directions.

DOWN IN THE VALLEY — Traditional

Down in the valley, the valley so low,
(F) (C_7)

Hang your head over, hear the wind blow;
(C_7) (F)

Hear the wind blow, dear, hear the wind blow,
(F) (C_7)

Hang your head over, hear the wind blow.
(C_7) (F)

Here are a number of other songs for harmonizing and following directions:

"Old Joe Clark." Directions:

(a) Play the F chord on the first word and on every steady beat for most of the song.
(b) Change to the C_7 chord for one beat at the words "come" (2nd line), "gone" (3rd line), and "Lucy" (4th line).

OLD JOE CLARK — Traditional

Went up on the mountaintop to give my horn a blow.
(F)

Thought I heard a pretty gal say, "Yonder comes my beau."
(F) (C_7) (F)

Fare you well, Old Joe Clark, fare you well, I'm gone.
(F) (C_7)

Fare you well, Old Joe Clark. Goodbye, Lucy Long.
(F) (C_7) (F)

NOTE: Additional verses may be found in *Making Music Your Own,* Bk. 6, p. 10, or in *Exploring Music,* Bk. 5, p. 74.

"I Don't Mind" (*Silver Burdett Music,* Bk. 4, p. 79). Directions:

(a) Play two strokes on each chord, in the following sequence: F B♭ F C_7.

(b) Play this sequence throughout the song. Play two strokes in each measure.

NOTE: If the autoharp is not in tune with the recording, the class can learn the song, then sing it *without* the recording, and *with* the autoharp.

"He's Got the Whole World in His Hands." Directions:

(a) Play the G chord, four steady strokes, beginning with the *first* time "whole" is sung.
(b) Change to the D_7 chord for four steady strokes the *second* time the word "whole" is sung.
(c) Return to the G chord for the *third* "whole."
(d) Change to D_7 for the *fourth* "whole" for two strokes only.
(e) Play the G chord on the last word.

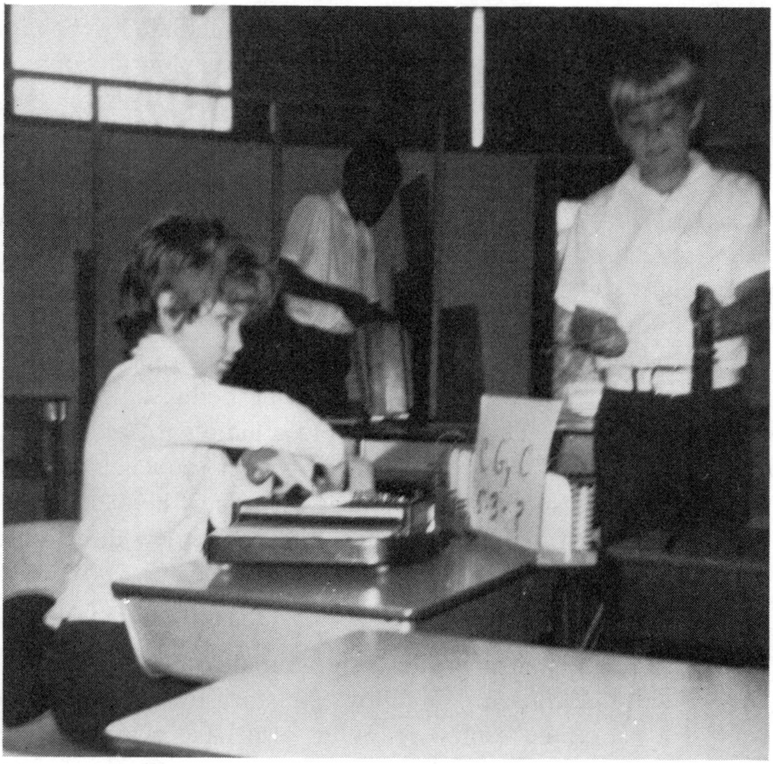

Fig. 9 Harmonizing with instruments

(*For the teacher:*)

HE'S GOT THE WHOLE WORLD IN HIS HANDS   Spiritual

He's got the whole world in his hands,
(G)
He's got the whole world in his hands,
(D_7)
He's got the whole world in his hands,
(G)
He's got the whole world in his hands.
(D_7)   (G)

NOTE: An alternate set of chords could be D and A_7. Make up additional verses for the song.

- **Remembering Verbal Sequences**

The study of geography has begun for intermediate level children. Listen to a song to remember sequences of geographic locations.

Geographic Sequences

Have the class listen carefully to the song "The City Blues" (*New Dimensions in Music,* Bk. 5, p. 6). Have a volunteer trace on a wall map the route to the eight cities mentioned in the eight verses of the song. (If eight verses are too many, use only the first four or five.) Have the children make up new verses with other city names.

Play a game by having the children prepare in advance a list of city or town names to fit into the song. One child sings his version while the class listens. Then another child attempts to trace the route from one city or town to the next, in the proper sequence, on a state or national map. A successful volunteer then sings his version and a new volunteer attempts to remember and trace the new directions.

- **Listening for the Main Idea**

Many composers have written programmatic music, that is, music that tells a story. Children can follow the story if they can perceive the central ideas of the composer. Songs also have a main idea that may not always be obvious without the composer's title. Try using the following orchestral and song materials to help develop the children's listening skills.

Fig. 10 Listening for the main idea

Programmatic Music

Play one of the following recordings:

"Royal March of the Lion" (Saint-Saëns, *Carnival of the Animals, New Dimensions in Music,* Bk. 4, Rec. 7)
"Under the Big Top" (Donaldson, *Bowmar Orchestral Library,* BOL #51)
"Sorcerer's Apprentice" (Dukas, *Bowmar,* #59)

Have the children discuss the sound-events they hear. Ask them to select titles the composer may have used that seem appropriate to the music. List the suggested titles as they are given, and after the class chooses one, tell the children the real title the composer gave to his work.

NOTE: Other suggestions are:

"Winter Holiday" (Prokofiev, *RCA Adventures in Music,* Gr. 3, Vol. 2)
"Embryonic Journey" (Jefferson Airplane, *Surrealistic Pillow,* RCA Victor)

Songs for Titles

The following songs have titles less obvious and more sophisticated than those for younger children. Do not give the children the titles in advance.

"Dust of Snow" (*Exploring Music,* Bk. 5, p. 64)
"Black and Gold" (*Magic of Music,* Bk. 6, p. 84)
"Mountain Sound" (*Silver Burdett Music,* Bk. 5, p. 150)

Sing the song, or play the recording of it, then list the children's suggestions for an appropriate title to fit the main ideas expressed in the text. After the class chooses one of these, tell them the real name of the song. Discuss the differences in their and the composer's choice.

• Listening for Sound Sources and Their Meanings

Listening Chart

Ask the children to pay careful attention to the sounds around them, in order to build effective listening habits. Have them keep a listening chart on the bulletin board where they can record during the day:

Sounds I Heard	*The Sound Sources*
1. walking	1. peoples' feet
2. motor running	2. typewriter in the principal's office

Characteristics of the Sound

1. thumping
2. humming, low, smooth

Vary the activity by having each student keep a chart of his own listening experiences during a given period of time. Have a chart on the bulletin board to represent a summary of the individual records.

Silent Times

1. Periodically call for complete silence in the room so that the class can listen to the surrounding sounds. Have one student report quickly on one of the sounds he hears. Help the others classify the

sound according to source, dynamics, pitch, and duration. Have a class recorder keep a general record.

2. After several sessions, discuss with the class the sounds they heard, the significance of each sound to their own living experience, the kind of listening it requires, and the frequency with which it is heard. Why are some sounds more important than others? Do some sounds change in importance because of differing circumstances?

3. Use the discussions as seeds for written compositions and for creative musical composing with tape recorder.

Useful Resources

The following materials have been referred to in the preceding lesson ideas and are recommended as helpful resources for the classroom.

BASIC ELEMENTARY SERIES BOOKS WITH RECORDINGS

Discovering Music Together, by Charles Leonard *et al.* Chicago: Follett Publishing Company, 1970, Bks. 2, 4, 5, 7.

Exploring Music, by Eunice Boardman and Beth Landis. New York: Holt, Rinehart & Winston, Inc., 1971, Bks. 2 and 5.

Growing with Music, by Harry R. Wilson *et al.* Englewood Cliffs, N.J.: Prentice-Hall, Inc., 1970, Bk. 2.

The Magic of Music, by Lorraine Watters, *et al.* Boston: Ginn and Company, 1971, Bks. 3 and 6.

Making Music Your Own, by Beatrice Landeck, Elizabeth Crook, and Harold C. Youngberg. Morristown, N.J.: Silver Burdett Company, 1971, Bks. 2, 4, 5, 6.

New Dimensions in Music, by Robert Choate *et al.* Cincinnati: American Book Company, 1970, Early Childhood, Bks. 2, 3, 4, 5, 6.

Silver Burdett Music, by Elizabeth Crook, Benett Reimer, and David S. Walker. Morristown, N.J.: Silver Burdett-General Learning Corporation, 1974, Bks. 1, 4, 5, 6.

The Spectrum of Music, by Mary Val Marsh *et al.* New York: The Macmillan Company, Inc., 1974, Bks. 2, 3, 4, 6.

RECORD COLLECTIONS AND OTHER RECORDINGS

Bowmar Orchestral Library, Bowmar Records, Inc. BOL #51, 53, 59, 60, 70.

RCA Adventures in Music Series, RCA Victor, LE1000, Grade 3, Vols. 1 and 2; Grade 6, Vol. 1.

Activities for Individualization in Movement and Music, H. Glass (Educational Activities, Inc., AR49).

Aretha Franklin (Columbia Records, GT-31355).

Berg: Chamber Concerto (Connoisseur Record Corporation, PLPS624).

Carole King Music, Carole King (A&M Records, ADE-SP77103).

Carole King Tapestry, Carole King (A&M Records, ODE-SP77009).

Chicago Three, James William Guercio (Columbia Records, C2-30110).

Coleman Hawkins, Archive of Folk Music and Jazz (Everest Records, FS-252).

Colors of the Day, Judy Collins (Elektra Records, EKS-75030).

The Concert for Bangladesh, George Harrison and Phil Spector (Apple, STCX3385).

Great Russian Masterpieces (Vox Productions, Inc. VSPS 10/5).

Happy Folk Dances, Michael Herman Folk Dance Orchestra (RCA Victor, LPM-1620).

If You Love Me, Olivia Newton-John (MCA Records, MCA-411).

Instruments of the Orchestra, National Symphony Orchestra (RCA Victor, LES6000).

Love Is Blue, Living Marimbas (RCA Camden, CAS-2253).

Music in Today's Classroom, Recordings for, accompanying text by Lois Rhea Land and Mary Ann Vaughn (Harcourt Brace Jovanovich, Columbia Records, CSP-P4-11611).

My Favorite Concertos, Van Cliburn (RCA, RK-1201).

Parsley, Sage, Rosemary, and Thyme, Simon and Garfunkel (Columbia Records, CS9363).

The Pines of Rome, Respighi, London Symphony Orchestra (Everest, 3051).

Scherchen Conducts Music for Multiple Orchestras, Beethoven, "Victory Symphony" (ABC Records, Inc., MS-801).

Sounds of New Music (Folkways, FX 6160).

Stevie Wonder Innervisions, Stevie Wonder (Tamla Records, T-326V1).

Teaser and the Firecat, Cat Stevens (A&M Records, SP4313).

The Worst of Jefferson Airplane, Jefferson Airplane (RCA, LSP 4459).

BOOKS

Active Learning: Games to Enhance Academic Abilities, Bryant L. Cratty (Englewood Cliffs, N.J.: Prentice-Hall, Inc., 1971).

Change for Children: Ideas and Activities for Individualizing Learning, Sandra Nina Kaplan *et al.* (Pacific Palisades: Goodyear Publishing Company, Inc., 1973).

Mankind in Time and Place, Kenneth S. Cooper, Clarence W. Sorensen, Lewis Paul Todd (Morristown, N.J.: Silver Burdett-General Learning Corporation, 1972).

Melody, Movement and Language, Millie Burnett (San Francisco: R & E Research Associates, 1973).

MMCP Synthesis, Ronald B. Thomas (Bardonia, N.Y.: Media Materials, Inc., 1971).

Modern Math Made Easy, Rose Broudy (New York: Harvey House, Inc., 1970).

Music and Movement Improvisations, Miriam Stecher, Hugh McElheny, and Marion Greenwood (New York: The Macmillan Co., 1972).

The Silver Burdett Elementary Science Program, George G. Mallinson *et al.* (Morristown, N. J.: Silver Burdett-General Learning Corporation, 1972).

PERIODICALS

"Integrative Symmetry in Music and Science," Donald Hatch Andrews, *Main Currents in Modern Thought,* Vol. 27, No. 5, May/June, 1971, pp. 147–156.

"Let's Not Only Get Their Attention," James O'Brien, *Music Educators Journal,* December, 1972, pp. 30–31.

"The Symbolic Arts: Humanism Through the Curriculum of the Symbol," J. Jack Manuel, *Music Educators Journal,* November, 1974, 38–42.

"The Thought-Life of the Young Child," Sister Cecilia Schmitt, *Music Educators Journal,* December, 1971, pp. 22–26.